Running
in Darkness

ROBERT CURRIE

COTEAU
BOOKS

Edited by Geoffrey Ursell.
Cover and book design by Duncan Campbell.

Cover image: "Swings in Mist," by Erik Rank, Photonica Collection/Getty Images

Printed and bound in Canada at Gauvin Press.
The interior of this book is printed on FSC certified paper, 100% recycled.

Library and Archives Canada Cataloguing in Publication

FSC

Recycled
Supporting responsible
use of forest resources

Cert no. SGS-COC-2624
www.fsc.org
© 1996 Forest Stewardship Council

Currie, Robert, 1937-
    Running in darkness / Robert Currie.

Poems.
ISBN 1-55050-351-0

I. Title.
PS8555.U7R85 2006   C811'.54   C2006-903074-X

2 3 4 5 6 7 8 9 10

COTEAU BOOKS

2517 Victoria Ave.
Regina, Saskatchewan
Canada S4P 0T2

Available in Canada and the US from:
Fitzhenry & Whiteside
195 Allstate Parkway
Markham, Ontario
Canada L3R 4T8

The publisher gratefully acknowledges the financial assistance of the Saskatchewan Arts Board, the Canada Council for the Arts, the Government of Canada through the Book Publishing Industry Development Program (BPIDIP), Association for the Export of Canadian Books, the Government of Saskatchewan, through the Cultural Industries Development Fund, and the City of Regina Arts Commission, for its publishing program.

This book is for Gwen,
for Bronwen, Darryl, Marin, and Brendan
for Ryan, Sharla, Jayden, and Joel,
with love.

contents

BEGINNING

BEGINNING AGAIN

ENDING

"Poetry.
I like to think of it
as statements made on the way to the grave."
— DYLAN THOMAS

Beginning

ONE WINTER NIGHT

In the pinched heart of the Depression,
at the arid prairie's edge: Furness, Saskatchewan.
The gaunt shadow of the United Grain Growers elevator
falls across the two-room shack beyond the town,
its tin roof, tin walls shaken in December wind.

Outside, spindly Russian thistle rattles,
frozen, holding down a thin drift of snow,
its brittle crust dark with dust from dry
summer-fallow on the grim hillside,
wind lashing along the ridge.

In the shack the elevator agent huddles
against his wife on a thirty-nine-inch bed,
frost clinging to its metal frame.
Curled beneath Hudson's Bay blankets,
he wraps her in his arms, listens
to a thrumming sheet of tin.

When the agent speaks, his words drift
on frozen breath and sink, chill
drafts shifting through the room.
It will get better, he tells her, next year,
there'll be grain to buy, next fall, he says,
next September, just you wait and see.
Above the headboard of the bed, tape
curls away from frosted window panes.

His gentle hands admire
her breasts, her slender thighs.
A frail moon shines like a broken icicle,
the tin house shivers on the bare plain,
and the moaning now is more than wind.
When they cry out, one after the other,
do they sense already I am on my way,
another reason to crave and fear September?

THE FAMILY IN BLACK AND WHITE

Jackpines bent by wind,
whitecaps frozen on stilled waves,
an empty beach beyond the checkered blanket

where we huddle together for the snapshot,
my mother wrapped in a dark cardigan, eyes
like anthracite, arm curled around my bare back.

I'm trying my best to smile, gazing
at my father bent above the camera.
His shadow stretches toward us,

like the outline of a giant stork,
head lowered, shoulders bunched,
my sister barely visible beneath the cardigan,

the whole family longing
for the day of her arrival.

It's the only picture of the four of us.

IN HIS PLACE

Wanting to talk, wanting a place in their conversation, I sit with my cookie and milk at the kitchen table, between them, my mother and the neighbour from three doors down, the two of them breathless with words streaming while jasmine tea cools in china cups from the sideboard, and knock knock, I whisper, the neighbour pausing to look, my mother shaking her head, no, go on, you were saying, but knock knock, I try again, my mother reaching with her right hand, vermillion nails floating toward me, dipping, and her hand falls on my lips, gentle as the petals of roses. Razor who, I say, the hand pressing tighter, squeezing, stopping my mouth. I look down at my glass of milk, lift it, turn it upside down on the table, milk gushing, submerging the pattern of pink impatiens in the plastic tablecloth, a white flood spreading, my mother and the lady from three doors down leaping from their seats, but silent at last, lifting the tablecloth by its edges – too late: the milk a river pouring into my lap. Razor hand if you want to talk, I say, and I stare down at my dress pants, soaked, my good shoes, awash in a puddle of milk, while I begin to quake, shattered by tears I didn't expect and cannot stop.

LIGHTNING

My father shapes the horse's head
with a fret saw, flaring nostrils,
pointed ears, files the splinters
from a broken rake handle, joins
the two with glue and nails, works
them over with number 5 sandpaper, grooming
the wood like a palomino's hide; my mother
unrolls her ball of light brown wool,
snips 8-inch lengths, with milliner's tape
attaches them to the bronc's curved neck.
While she braids leather boot laces
for a hackamore, I use my tempera paints
to make his coat the gold of sunlight, his eyes
the shade of black I know his hooves would be.

When I ride out, the city streets
fill with cactus, mesquite and snorting
long-horned steers, outlaws drain
their beers, leap on mustangs for the chase,
spurs rake heaving sides, reins beat haunches,
but Lightning surges beneath me, hooves
raging, his mane in my face, nothing
can catch us, till at last we make it safely
to the Pantry Shelf Confectionery
and I exchange my mother's dime
for our daily loaf of bread.

FRIEND OF THE FAMILY

Lips vibrating an engine's growl,
I run the Massey-Harris through gravel ruts,
pull grass by the front gate, pile it in a stack
till the screen door slams, and here comes Mr. Tierney
striding from my grandma's house,
a quarter flashing in his calloused hand.
He makes me a deal, the hay stack for the quarter,
invites me to spend the night at the farm, to bunk
in the room with his son who drives a real tractor.

His son's too busy to play, and that afternoon I design
in the sandpile a pattern of roads and trails
linking farms and pastures, excavate an alkali slough,
fill it with water scooped from the barn trough.
He calls me for supper, and I sit by his son,
a badge of tractor grease on his left knee.

When Mr. Tierney shuts his eyes and starts to talk,
I see his wife duck her head, his son bite
his lip and shift quickly away from me.
What's going on? I wonder, but Mr. Tierney's eyes
stay shut, and above his head a man and a woman stare
from a heavy frame, collars so tight they can't smile.

Beside them, a wooden cross, and on the far wall
a picture of Christ, thorns on his forehead, dirt
and sweat, blood running toward his eyes, blood
dripping from holes in the palms of his hands
– Oh jeez, he's talking to Christ!

Beyond the window his John Deere sits, the lugs
on its tires the size of my arms, and I
would give that tractor, the whole farm,
for the sofa-bed in my grandmother's porch.

YOUNG BOY, FLEEING

I remember running out pyjama-clad to the backstep.
Mrs. Loverin, our neighbour across the alley fence,
wheeled from hanging her Monday wash.
I'd been sick with fever, asleep in my parents' room,
the black oak desk beyond the bed, crooked
light from the cracked window, the dark cubby-hole

where the letter-opener gleamed a warning.
My chosen dinner finished, brown sugar, sweet
and golden, all of it spooned away, a thin layer
of Sonny Boy cereal congealed in the curve of the bowl,
I woke to the rumble of waves, blankets rumpled,
rolling toward me, raging wool waves

foaming over my face, pulling me under.
I flailed and twisted, fought free, ran past my aproned mother,
her hands in the sink, slicing the skin from potatoes.
Wrenching the door wide – shock
of cold boards on bare feet – I screamed
and screamed, They're going to kill me help me please.

Mrs. Loverin, a wooden clothespin caught in her teeth,
her puckered face like that of her budgie, a seed in its beak,
one sock dangling, her basket of clothes dropped in the dirt
as she turned to me with a look I'd never seen,
and behind me my mother, my loving innocent mother,
faltered at the door, the knife ablaze in her hand.

SLEEPOVER

Robbie tells his folks he's big enough.
His dad brings him giant packing boxes,
corrugated cardboard a quarter-inch thick.
Robbie hammers cardboard onto two-by-fours
while above his head the bigger boys
raise the tin roof of a Coca-cola sign.

They spread their sleeping bags that night
in the shadows of their amazing shack,
the yard beyond the empty doorway
drifting at last from dusk to dark.
They crawl outside. Look up.
A slice of moon, a splash of distant stars,
and closer, the flicker of moving lights,
a small plane murmurs through the night.

Back inside they talk about the ghost
that shakes the attic floor of Mrs. Martin's house,
the vampire bats that always swoop at midnight.
Shivers sweet along his spine. Then he curls
into his sleeping bag and drops away, never hears
the bigger boys creep outside, never knows
they're chased by old man Gibbs. Secure again
within their cardboard walls, they snap
fresh carrots with their teeth
while Robbie never stirs.

With the hum of morning traffic he awakes,
wonders how the guys can sleep so late.
Gets up. Feels the excitement of the night.
He ducks through the doorway, sees
his dad strolling down the lane.
His fifth trip since nine last night.

"It was great," Robbie says. "You just wouldn't believe
the fun we had. I barely slept at all."

THE REMINDER

Like a grown man, at work in the basement,
I'm splitting kindling for the furnace,
each log centred on the chopping block,
the blade aimed precisely for a centre line
that for a second I can almost see.
The hatchet is mine to use, the axe
waiting for my father's hand.
But oh, the fresh smell of sliced wood,
the sheen of grain just released to light.

Left hand holding, right hand swinging,
I cleave the logs with swift strokes,
cutting each piece again, again, again,
lean twins springing from the scarred block.
The next chop strikes my index finger knuckle,
a piece of flesh lopped off, blood spurting,
and I holler for Mom to bring a bandage.
"You're going to have a scar," she whispers,
"a small reminder to be more careful."

Looking at the scar today, noting
how it's edged to the left, resting now
in the hollow between my knuckles,
what I remember over five decades later
is a crying boy seated on the chopping block,
his mother kneeling motionless before him,
my left hand held in both of hers, the throbbing
eased by the warmth of her palms, the soothing
words, her breath a balm mingling with my own.

EVERY ONE OF US

On the top floor of King Edward School,
we sit in our desks, heads bent
over our times-tables, Miss Dunlop
before us as fierce as a badger.
"You'll stay in your seats," she says,
"every last one of you. Understood?"

The principal has canceled recess.
No one is permitted outside
until the schoolyard poplar is down.

We can hear the snarl and snap of a chainsaw,
so much like the rasp of Miss Dunlop
who has only to say, "Sit up straight!"
and instantly our backbones grow an inch.

"Eyes on your arithmetic books," she says,
and we bow before the one woman of her time
who will rise to the rank of principal.
Fleet glances from the left corner of our eyes.
"Five times five is twenty-five," we say,
"five times six is thirty."
                              The crack
of wood breaking, and we bolt as one,
scrambling over desks to the window, a single word
hot in every mouth: "Timber!" And the tree
leans away, leaning farther and faster, shaking,
till it falls, branches snapping, bouncing once, a fountain
of dust, settling back, leaves shivering, and we
discover ourselves pressed to the glass,

while behind us at the front of the room
Miss Dunlop looms from her desk,
no trace of a smile on her lips
as she leans slowly toward us,
the room filling with limbs
about to fall.

UNCLE ANDREW

"When he was your age," my aunt said,
"your uncle never once brushed his teeth."
Every night and in the evenings playing crib
he kept both plates in a shaving mug by the bed.

I used to grin when he relaxed, his mouth closing,
elastic lips collapsing back upon themselves,
the jut of his chin all but touching his nose,
but my aunt turned from the cards and shook her head.

He looked after me once while she was out at bingo.
I chuckled at the way his lips opened and folded
around the bottle he pulled from a brown paper bag.
"You think something's funny here?" he asked.

He set his bottle down and leaned toward me,
the slap like a two-by-four against my cheek.
I started to cry and ran for the bedroom.
"Stay there," he said, "or I'll cut off your cock."

It was hours before I fell asleep on the damp pillow.
When I awoke my uncle had already gone to work,
the aroma of cinnamon buns calling me to the kitchen.
I stayed at the bathroom mirror, brushing and brushing my teeth.

SUMMER AT MIDNIGHT

I read *Tom Sawyer*, read *Huck Finn*, a flashlight under the blankets while the house cools, creaks in the night, and my parents fall asleep, then I creep from my basement room, crawl through the coal chute window, prop it open. On tiptoes past my parents' window and a dash down the street, skirting the light from the lamp at the corner, the gravel of Iroquois Street rattling under my runners. I stoop for a handful of pebbles, race on. Breath like fire in my chest, I stop at the squeaky gate, pull it open the quiet eight inches, squeeze through. No light in the house of the McNabb boys. By the front window I can hear their father snoring. On the east side of the house I push through the hollyhocks, begin flicking pebbles at the screen. *Thung. Thung.* A face in the glass like the moon's reflection. I reach up, catch the screen as Rod unhooks it, Rod and Ralph wiggling out, dropping into the soft earth of the flowerbed. Together we sneak down the alley, the night air cool, a whisper of wind stirring with spirits. Bats wheel over Mrs. Salthammer's poplars, dive by our heads. Not a car moving on Main Street, but north of us in the C.P.R. yards an engine whistles, a train going somewhere in the night. We walk past dark and silent houses, here a fan blowing the curtains in a corner room, there a radio playing, Hank Williams wailing of lonesome railway crossings. Twice, cars turn the corner, their lights picking up only the caragana hedges where we have hidden. Everything altered by night, we walk the streets for hours, Ralph, who is ten, a spasm of shivers and giggles, ducking from sight at least four times to pee in the weeds. Yes, but our echoing footsteps proclaim that these are our streets. We own the night.

BEHIND MCBRIDE'S

In that last brief hour before our parents called us home
we sometimes strode the side-streets of South Hill,
eight or ten of us, girls and guys together, arms stretched
over shoulders, swaying down the centre of the street.
Neighbours on their porches paused at dusk from rocking,
listened to the latest lyrics from Alberta Slim,
approximations of his twang quavering in our throats.
Those nights, as the sky shifted into shadow, stars humming
beneath the minstrel moon, Jack Schultz, who lived a block away,
neither sang our songs, nor felt our arms across his back.

We always kept our distance, frightened by the temper
of the toughest kid in King Edward School.
Then one day Reg took him on at noon hour,
behind McBride's Store, out of sight of any teacher,
a circle of kids jammed around the two of them
exchanging blows, thumping shoulders, chests, bellies,
puffing and grunting, punching harder, until Reg
swung wildly, caught Schultz in the face, a sound
like a wooden shingle snapping, a spray of blood,

Schultz's mouth dropping open, hanging open,
while he was struck again, and he spun away,
clawed an opening in the wall of hushed kids
who stared at one another, breathless, stunned,
then turned to follow him, chanting his name.
Blood gushed from his broken nose. He fled
down the centre of the street, a pack of hooting kids
running now, howling, as we chased him home,
our taunts beating down like the hot noon sun.

EVERYBODY KNEW

Annie, a grade behind me in school,
as sure as September sent by her father,
ten dollar bill in the sleeve of her blouse,
shuffled to our back door, one hand clenched.

Before her hesitant knock, I'd spend hours
searching for bent pages to straighten, erasing pencil
smudges like bruises, taping gashes, my textbooks
restored, looking undamaged, almost untouched,

and sold for less than they'd bring
from any other kid on the block.
As if somehow that would satisfy her father
and keep him from his daughter's bed.

PLAYING CATCH

I'm working on my curveball.
My father plays without a crouch,
his joints stiff with rheumatism,
cane hooked in his back pocket,
both hands freed for the catch.

He jerks his shins, blocks
the balls beneath his awkward reach.
His throws whip back to me,
burst into my glove, all the motion
from his muscled arm.

He tells me snap my wrist more,
make it break below his knees.

THE GIFT

The best Christmas present ever
comes in grade eight, an RCA record player;
it holds a stack of forty-fives, is silent
until wired into my Silvertone mantel radio.
With the door closed in my basement room,
one after the other, the records drop,
the Four Aces give way to the Ames Brothers,
the Four Lads, the Crewcuts, while I sway
and gaze at the dresser mirror, yearning
for three brothers to join me, belting out
    Heart of My Heart,
      Hoop-De-Doo,
       Istanbul (Not Constantinople),
        Crazy 'bout Ya, Baby,
a rolled copy of *Maclean's* clutched
in my hand for a microphone, already
knowing that some dreams are worth
little, my voice an engine
spinning its tires, not one lick
like a tune, no idea how
lucky I am, other songs,
dynamic energy straining
and surging inside, words
and sounds wanting out,
absolutely no way yet
to let them go.

FALLING

April 8th, 1954
for Larry

When we rode our bikes
to school that day,
we didn't know
there'd soon be people
stopped on busy cross-walks
staring at the sky, the Harvard trainer
colliding with the North Star which twisted
down, the pilot's knuckled hands
holding it above the elementary
school, thirty-five people drawing
sudden breaths, the bigger plane
bursting open, a silver wing
sliding off, the explosion
plunging passengers into the exhibition
grounds, the golf course, the back
yard of a woman hanging
out her wash, flames like water
pouring down, the fusilage
shattering a house, another woman
working there, a cleaning woman is
what the papers said, but no, they got it
wrong, she wasn't that, she was
the mother of my friend
and she was dead that morning,
the very day we rode
our bikes to school,
pumping hard, lifting
off the curbs, a breathless
instant in the air

RESULTS
for Ralph

In those days we wanted quick results.
The chemicals not for sale, we stole.
Your brother working at the drug store
did deliveries after school, pedaling
home with vials of what we needed.

We hack-sawed six inch sections
from plumber's pipe, packed them full.
Began on the prairie, miles from town.
Rejoicing at results, earth
and sky transposed, we rolled
in mirth upon the hot grass.
Next, the corner confectionery.
Between the storm and inner doors
we squatted with a match, lit
the fuse, bolted for the alley.
The sound like a bomb in a tunnel.

We had no thought for broken glass,
cracked doors, the one customer,
Mrs. Crocker, with her bag of red licorice,
departing at the wrong time.
No thought for ourselves
crimping fuses, squeezing nitrates

until the day that you
tamped in the final grains,
tapped them once too often,
your hand burst around the blast,
you ran screaming on the lawn,
its bright green spattered with red,
with bits of you, your other hand
untouched, the hand that one day
would earn your living as an artist.

JUBILEE

The year we went to California was 1955,
my summer beneath a coat of Clearasil.
Before we started that July, my father
acquired three hundred paper matchbooks,
each bearing three sheaves of wheat,
a gilded windblown banner proclaiming
"Saskatchewan's Golden Jubilee."
He planned to celebrate along the way,
to let the Americans know about our home.
"Pop," I said, cringing in the back seat,
"nobody's gonna want your stupid penny matches."
What I meant, of course, was Don't embarrass me.

From the Montana border to the San Francisco Bay
he gave them out every time we stopped,
to gas jockeys, waitresses, motel clerks,
to every chance passer-by in every whistle-stop.
They responded with handshakes, extra fries,
soft drink refills, with etched souvenir glasses
in Salt Lake City; colored prints of western scenes
in Winnemucca; with rolls of nickels for
the Reno slot machines. Through the windshield
I watched the transformations, faces
masked for work, open and alive again.
Everywhere we stopped, they stopped,
suspended from the day, smiling, wondering
if we knew their cousins in Vancouver,
if we'd had much snow this summer,
if he'd say that Saska-word again.

In Redding, California, I saw a girl my age,
a pert brunette, peroxide streaked hair.
She looked as cool as the peak of Mount Shasta,
and just as distant, far too cute for me,
but I slid from the backseat. "Pop," I said,
"those matches, could I maybe have a few?"

P.S. Her name was Merrilee. For three incredible
years her letters bound California to Saskatchewan.
Thanks, Pop. Thanks a million.

THE LAST TIME

I'm twenty minutes late again,
the other students floating
on a sea of similes, a rising tide of words.
I push the door open, late slip in hand,

Miss Seymour stranded in a poem I've never heard,
a sound of ocean ebbing in the room,
her students gasping, flopping on a reef
that's risen, stark and rocky,

through the swell of imagery.
She glares at me, head shaking,
her eyes as sharp as broken shells.
I cannot meet those eyes, I look away,

look down at her loose fitting cotton blouse,
one of ten shapeless tops that make it possible
for me to occupy the same room with her.
"Young man," she says, "your interruptions

are destructive. They have to stop."
I feel her eyes on mine. I see
her left hand slowly rise,
flutter an instant at her neck

before her fingers light upon her collar button,
her thumb beneath the figured fabric,
two fingers flick and tug above,
the emerald button plucked free.

"For your sake too, I want you here. The whole hour,"
her voice husky, rough as coral. Her fingers
descend again, another button falling free,
another and another, a sigh of fabric parting.

"There are some things," she says,
"that you must simply get beyond."
The last button undone, she pulls the blouse open,
shrugs her shoulders, milky skin, a trace of pink,

the blouse falls away, breathless white satin,
a lace margin stretches stunningly, her hands
behind her back, she bends slightly at the waist,
the satin bra drops.

"I pray you're worth this," her voice low and luminous,
flowing, a murmur of waves, her breasts
float before me, nipples dark as starfish.
"And now," she says, "let's get back to 'Dover Beach.'"

And then, among her students, all of whom
— like me — at last begin to breathe again,
I take my place, transformed, knowing
two prayers were answered here.

AWAY GAME
    for Clink and Flash

This happened so long ago
a touchdown was worth just five points.
Our high school team took a chartered bus
down the Soo Line for a game at Notre Dame,
not, of course, the fabled fighting Irish,
who, hearts warmed by Coach Rockne's fire,
once burnt the odds and triumphed for the Gipper.

No, these were merely prairie boys, Roman Catholics
mainly, but not much different from ourselves.
When our bus rolled past the Paterson elevator,
we saw the broad Main Street of Wilcox,
a row of false fronts, peeling clapboard boxes.
Someone took us to a student dorm,
up warped wooden stairs thick with dried gumbo,

past a jumble of muddy shoes,
stack after stack of food-encrusted dishes,
over floors with litter scattered everywhere.
The windows, though, were clean
as sunshine, clear as autumn air.
Who'd believe it? Not a pane of glass in all of them.
We shivered in those chilly rooms, thinking

these guys, man, they sure must be tough.
We hurried into football gear, a steady rhythm,
the pounding of leather on leather outside.
Rushing to the windows, we saw a double row
of linemen stretched across Main Street,
crouched an instant, driving hard at one another,
then calisthenics, push-ups, players striding in the air,

tight formations running plays, churning up the dust
while half-tons idled in the middle of the street.
Later, at the football field, a grassy pasture,
its yardlines and gopher holes marked by paint,
we heard from sixty yards away
the full bellow of Father Athol Murray
preaching hell-fire to his Catholic boys

who that long ago September day
went out and beat us thirty-six to zip.
Annihilation, yes, humiliation, sure,
but young and green as spring
we learned one thing that day:
the heart is always in the mind,
it's all that ever matters.

THE DANCE
(circa 1956)

Wham Bam a Bam Bam
a Bop Bam Boom
No sense no need
for sense at all
just music
pushing at the dark
Jerry Lee Little Richard
Elvis knock it out
until you feel it
throbbing in your skin
Rammy Sammy Ohhh Mammy
Your feet begin to move
driven by the beat
you twist and spin
pulse of song and blood
shake away the day
set something free
Rammy Sammy Ohhh Mammy
The music and its trance
making you
the dance
YEAH

SOME PLACES I'VE BEEN,
SOME REASONS I MADE IT THIS FAR

Beyond the village of Hendon, Saskatchewan, the dry fall of '43, I
lie in a grassy ditch with my chin in my hands and watch
the fire. Flames jump in the wind, a frenzy of wildfire
sweeping over the field. In my right hand I clutch the
stolen packet of matches.

South of Moose Jaw, I help the Boughen twins stack sections of
CNR snow-fence into piles we lug away from the tracks
and tumble over the river bank. An engine belching
smoke and curses, we dig in our heels and slide, pebbles
and stones leaping beneath our feet. Safe by the river we
build our rafts for the spring rise of '51.

On 31st Street in Saskatoon, the boarder who fought in the war
tells me to hang on tight and guns his shiny '46 Harley
toward the stop sign on Avenue A. Wind in my mouth
and I know we'll never be able to stop. I shudder and pray
he'll go faster, faster.

In the town of Furness, Boots, the black terrier with white legs,
sinks his teeth in the tail of my jumper and drags me
toward the tin house by the elevator. He pulls me back
again and again. When what I want this long afternoon of
1940 is to walk all the way to Neville Goss's General Store
and Post Office. Where the German helmet hangs on the
wall and Mr. Goss sits on his wooden stool, a green patch
over the hole where his eye used to be.

On the gravel road between Paynton and Maidstone, late July of
'54, Uncle John lets me drive the Ford coupe he won at
the Battleford fair. I press on the gas. Tires burning the
sharp turn at the slough where every summer the tourists
die, he grabs the wheel and somehow holds us on the road.

In the middle aisle of Moose Jaw's new Metropolitan store, the
        boring August of 1948, I show Tim Davies the genuine
        cowhide Roy Rogers rodeo wallet on the pocketbook
        counter. We look beyond the countertops, up and down
        the empty aisle. I slip out of the store with fire on my hip.

Along the private road where the cops seldom check, Clink and
        Chenny, Flash and I drive in the winter of '57. Clink
        parks the car beside a snow bank in shadows thrown by
        the rusting tanks of Husky Oil. We nod our heads and
        open the forty of Scotch.

Crouched in the lane behind 32nd Street, the chill autumn of
        1945, I lean against the garage, hold the match to a
        splinter of clapboard siding. A hand falls on my shoulder.
        The man drags me home by my burning ear, dust
        smoking from under my feet as I strain to keep up.

HICK

The college girls
seemed imports
from a foreign world

His English prof
charting novels at the board
never wore a bra
and he knew he blushed
when she mentioned phallic symbols
Once she caught him   circled
hovered   as she spoke
            Take Hemingway's *The Sun Also Rises*
            The name   Robert Cohn   Surely you can see it
            Might we have some symbolism there?

While other students
turned to look
    the girls   the smiling girls
he felt that he
was everybody's fool
            Cajones   Surely
            you see it now   Cajones
            You might just explain
            the significance of that

            Certainly   You're the one
            I'm talking to

The blood rushing to his face
he groped for any kind of mask
            Back home he said there's cows an bulls
            but I'd have to say
            your Mr. Cohn was a steer
His mouth   dry as straw

CAMPUS PARTY

Oh man he wished he hadn't come   his blood
was thin his hand trembled on the mug
and all around him guys were saying
witty things that made him laugh
at just the wrong time   he laughed
and had another beer   someone
in the corner flogging a piano
the singers grouped like prayer *Do Lord*
Oh do Lord oh do remember me
he knew that he could play it better
if his hands would play if his hand
wasn't sticking to a mug of beer
he drank and joined the swaying
circle   hanging on the edge the song
turning *way beyond the sea*
some day he'd have a home in glory land
and everyone would hear him play
wet   his head was wet   someone pouring
beer   when he turned   no one was there
a beer fight slopped across the room
he had another drink   the floor
turning   tilted   and he lost his balance
fell in beer that ran like slaughter
house blood   an accident
that faces watched   he could not rise
still   he wasn't any carcass on the floor
he pulled himself outside   away
drifting snow wind peeling the snow
away   somehow he'd get away

THE SUMMER I WORKED CONSTRUCTION

Two hundred and seventy-six miles from Moose Jaw
to Maidstone, but I was driving my father's car the wrong way,
weekend over, shovel and gravel waiting for Monday,
and you were there with your mom in the little house,
the cellar packed with darkness, trap door by the couch,
where I lay, thrilled by your quiet breathing,
– waves on a moonlit lake sliding to shore –
but here there was no moon, and you
were on the other side of the wall, though hand
in hand we'd walked out of town that evening,
puffs of dust rising together at every step,
hushed prairie and bush, one magpie in the dusk
just a whisper of black, gliding low
at the edge of vision, your shoulder
pressed against mine, we talked of when
we'd meet again, how we'd manage
our lives, wanting the magic to last, your hand
still in mine, though both of us knew it was over,
and here I was, back on the pavement, driving
through Paynton, the town I knew as a boy,
the grain elevator where my uncle worked in the '40s
burnished now by the sinking sun, no one knowing
that one day it would fall, collapsing,
a fury of splinters and dust, an expert
imported from somewhere else
to manage the blast.

WORKING ON THE NINNY-SPOON

Eight o'clock whistle goes,
sun already hot, shirt
sticking to my back.
I scoop dirt from the ditch,
don't fling it past my shoulder
like the new kid they hired.
There's eight hours today,
another eight tomorrow.
I try to get a rhythm going,
shovel down, into dirt,
up again, sweeping sideways,
easy lift, easy rhythm,
make it smooth as loafing
and I can think of other things,
going back to school this fall,
the jazz band again,
my horn to blow – yeah,
if my hands aren't forever
shaped by this shovel handle.
Ellington and Satchmo, a little scat,
yah bop a doo doo rah be bop,
slide into something classical,
donn donn donn de dahh.
If I open my mouth now
these guys'll hear a symphony.

I glance at my watch,
look away just in time,
push it under the cuff.
With the stiffness gone,
muscles greased, working smoothly,
got to be eight-thirty now.
Mustn't think about the time,
just keep the shovel going,
think of something –
Ow! Hit a rock. The handle
shakes through glove and callus,
strikes something tender in the palm.
My watch is down again.
I shove it up and out of sight,
dig carefully around the rock
like it's a bloody diamond.
Which in a way it is,
something different in the day.
It's a big one. I cut it loose,
take the weight with my legs,
lift it, swing it from the ditch,
set it gleaming roughly in the sun.
Back to dirt and more dirt,
start the rhythm once again.
Let the shovel do the work,
down, in, up, swing,
let the mind find a rhythm,
rah bop a bau bau,
yah do yah do yah do.
Write a score upon the clouds.
Yah do yah do wa waaa.
Summer wind and summer sky.
Yah do yah do da daaa.
Heaven's in my honey's eye.

Must be an hour now, more,
the sun higher, hotter,
the ditch longer, deeper.
And somehow still the same.
Sweat dropping on my glasses,
I clean them on my shirttail
and the world turns hazy.
I keep it that way,
a soft romantic haze,
think of sun glasses, beaches,
sand warm with sunshine,
girls in bathing suits,
water fresh and cool.
Big mistake. I'm thirsty now.
It must be nearly ten.
I do it right this time,
spit on each lens,
rub away the smudges,
the world once more in lines
sharp as a pick blade, sharp
as the architect's blue prints
of what we're going to build here.
No escape in that.
My watch slipping on a wrist
wet with morning sweat,
I try to push it up,
but I've already looked.
Eight-twenty. Shit.
Two hours I've slaved so far
and only twenty minutes gone.

THAT DAY

My afternoon class already cancelled,
I sat in our basement suite at noon,
making a sandwich, considering
which book to begin from those on my list,
but the radio was on – interruptions – and soon
I was spreading peanut butter on toast,
the knife moving senselessly back and forth
like a weather vane caught in a wind
that changes and changes again.

I left my lunch by the kitchen sink, walked out
to the '56 Chev, its tank nearly empty, drove
all the way across town to the gas station
whose owner once supplied my roommate and me
with buckets of used oil for our old junker
that burned black gold like a wildfire at the well.
Filled the tank there, a debt of loyalty,
though at first I thought the owner was gone,
his face like a stranger's, his hand on the pump
like an automaton – he didn't seem to remember or care.

All afternoon I drove through the city,
turning at corners I'd never seen,
streets I'd never known, rows of houses,
bungalows with white siding, exactly
the kind I might some day own, but now
they could all be awaiting the wrecker's ball,
their groomed lawns stretching flat and lifeless,
like him, surrounded by rushing men, doctors
and agents, frantic for hope, his body
laid out on that gurney in Dallas.

CONTACT

In the U. of S. bookstore, pricing texts for intersession,
I'm drawn to a wire rack, a rugged face, slashes of red
and gold across a thoughtful visage. I seize
the book, the price so low I know for sure
there's been a grave mistake, I rush
to the till, fling down my cash before
some harried clerk can raise the price.
On the first bench outside I begin
A Red Carpet for the Sun.

Wandering in the stacks where I once lost
all my powers of concentration, finding
Desmond Pacey's *Creative Writing in Canada*
bookmarked with what seemed to be a snapshot
of the German actress, Maria Schell, her smile
enough to melt ice from January windshields,
today I spot a pamphlet, yellowed pages
bound by staples, *When We Are Young*.

Tonight I jot down an image, play
with words, try to give them shape.
There's been no official diagnosis,
but already I know I'm afflicted
with a fever that I pray will
rage through all my days.

Beginning Again

STARTING OUT TOGETHER
for Gwen

We brake and stop for a solitary moose,
its hulking shoulders, its dark bulk just visible
in a thrill of moonlight by the lake.
Then we hear our song on the car radio.

We're deep in the park, miles from the Narrows,
our honeymoon cabin where light dies at midnight,
the generator stilled, cold stars shaking above.
Car doors flung wide, we step out together,

dance on the band of broken pavement,
aspens quaking in the car's dim light,
beyond them, black woods, rock and decay,
the eyes of animals, awake and waiting.

Warm in each other's arms, aching with love,
through August air chilled by bitter wind
we sway together easy as a promise,
footsteps in concert, the thrum of music,

the reassuring hum of the idling engine,
shadows and moonlight, silent pines around us,
while somewhere, north of the park, an animal,
alone and in pain, tears at its paw in the dark.

SATURDAY MORNING

Sun bright in the driveway,
I shower her with water, strip
away the coat of dust, bare body
gleaming with beads of moisture,
I rub her down, shammy wild
in my hand, her figure sleek
and lubricious, warming
beneath my touch,
I stroke her
gleaming curves,
massage her
secret crevices,
sweat springs
from my pores,
runs between my
shoulder blades,
I press the arc
of her body, reach
and stroke, that marvelous
chassis firm and burning
beneath me, I buff
every inch of her, hot
chrome shining
          and you
at our bedroom window
rub sleep from your eyes,
ah, that smile is there,
slow, sensual,
         and I
am heading back to you.

MARILYN WANTS HELP

but I'm a first year teacher who knows
nothing about the Bryant Oratory Contest
except the speak-off comes in three weeks.
I read her speech twice, manage to suggest
a few changes that might matter just a bit.
Marilyn says she needs to practice, and I know
tomorrow's lesson planning will be finished
late tonight. We meet after school. I listen
to her speech, now and then her words
snap like struck matches, the empty room
crackles with scattered flames.

What help can I offer a grade eleven girl
who's a better speaker than her teacher?
"Pretend there's someone in every single desk.
Try to look at all of them as if they're friends."
Day after day I listen from the back of the room.
Yes, but she longs for oratorical advice.
I nod my head and wonder what to say.
"You've got a great smile, you know.
It wouldn't hurt to let the judges see it."

Marilyn is nervous. She wants help
she doesn't need. She needs to know
she's good at this. She won't
believe me when I tell her so.
Tomorrow and again I'll listen
to her speech. You know, Marilyn,
I think that you might win.
When the day arrives I think
she finally thinks so too.

2E

Every noon I resist pacing, sit in the corner
of the staff room, pray to keep my dinner down.
Stomach ties itself in tighter knots, acid
rising in my throat, the minute hand swings
toward the final bell – my slow walk up to 2E.

Ripped blinds in the windows, graffiti
around a hole in the wall, a glossary
of curses carved in the teacher's desk,
thirty-six grade tens whose only goal
seems to be an early end to my career.

Tough guys slouch on either side of the desk,
each of them named Randy – I stop them once
from fighting, fists like hammers, a girl
screaming. I suppose the one
they'd like to pound is me.

Every time I turn to scrawl a note on the blackboard,
whispers detonate silence, spitballs fly like shrapnel.
Every time I draw a conclusion, try to make a point,
Susan scowls, Shirley snaps her gum,
Ted and Peter sneer, Shelley talks to anyone.

Some days I think about the unemployment office,
wonder what better jobs might be posted there.
Every day I long for Christmas, a break
from school, and yes, peace on earth, but war
continues, every class a battle for attention.

When Christmas yields to January, I climb the stairs
to 2E, armed for more hostilities. Shelley talks
and touches on the subject, Shirley has her homework
nearly done, Peter sneers, sure, and Heather waves a hand
to answer, Richard's willing to elaborate.

Something here has changed, a treaty
signed, perhaps. The peace will be
uneasy, skirmishes frequent.
For the first time I surmise
we'll maybe all survive.

FIRST POEM FOR BRONWEN

A toy telephone
for my one-and-a-half-year-old
because she loves talking to Granny.
Her eyes shiver with delight.
Chubby fingers sweep phone to head.
"Hi, Danny. 's Bonnen"
A shadow across her eyes.
"Danny? ...Hi? ...Danny!"
Lips shudder,
a tear cutting her cheek.
Her eyes stab at me.
Deceived by her father,
the first betrayal.
Unintentional, sure,
but it won't be the last.

LEAN
AND
HUNGRY

If
I write
a

n
a
r
r
o
w

poem

lean
as a
famine

someday
I'll find
an editor
with
a space
about
|-this wide-|

then
you
fat guys
can sweat
in the
steam baths
while
I
move
in

MOVING OUT
(circa 1972)

Earle Birney's in Regina tonight
and we consider going
though the noon news moans storm warnings
and forty miles of February separate us.

Winter hulks huge
with icy brow
and fistfuls of snow.
But Birney beckons
from sunhot spires
and bloodied crags near Banff.
He moves out
from False Creek mouth:
– sliding past billboards,
blots that blast the hillsides,
– bouncing on buses
with men whose spewing mouths
run with a diarrhea
no diaper can stifle,
– soaring over a Canada
shaking free from pimpled adolescence,
– Birney   moving up and out
and in   on the world.

Tonight the evening glooms;
hanging clouds haunt prairie farms
which sulk beneath a shroud of snow
while, through the fog, their lights gleam
like the eyes of sullen wolves.
We move out, and the snow
swirls free from the pavement,
the highway's white line
lunging straight for the lectern.

FAME

Home from work, I discover the bundle from Delta,
eager to see my poems typeset, in print,
not spewed from my cranky old mimeo,
when my wife passes me, going out the door.
Heedless, I rip brown paper in a frenzy of excelsior.
"I've got to get downtown," she says, "before six.
Your son needs his pants changed."

Reluctantly flipping him diaper free,
I find a surly red butt
looking as if it had sat
in burnt scalloped potatoes,
and my three-year-old colour commentator
announces, "Ryan's got poop. He stinks."

Fingers that would touch
the crisp pages of my poems
now wring the neck of a diaper
and, hunched over the toilet bowl,
I ponder on that student today
who couldn't grasp the meaning of irony.

JUMP SHOT

Being shorter than the guy who covers me,
I need to play upon his mind, make him think
I'm driving to his right and going up, something
I've practised at least a thousand times,
the ball at my fingertips, footsteps
falling as perfectly as print upon a page
laying out the trail that leads to ambiguity,
so he tries to cut me off, stumbles,
and he is addled now, already in the air,
hands flapping at the fake, descending as I rise,
the ball beyond his outstretched hand, a prayer
that arcs toward the basket, the sibilant hiss of cords
so much like that modest gasp of breath
that sometimes attends the reading
of a lyric's final line.

THE EYES OF MAY

The sidewalks coloured with people
and Ryan perched on my knee
for the Kinsmen Band Festival.
His big eyes parade the street
looking for clowns with balloons
till a cannon cracks in his head
– the flypass of jets from the air base.

Eyes roll whitely, screams spilling like tears.
And I hadn't thought of a three-year-old's fright.
For a half hour after, he shakes,
his hands clamped to his head.

At home, he still flips his library book
grinning at pictures of pilots and planes,
but, outside, streaks for the back door,
moaning, hands beating his ears
to knock away a jet's distant wail.

This morning, he edges out the door,
surveys a blue sky soaked in sunshine,
circles the yard, warily,
then bounds to his mother's side:
"Nice day, Mom! No air planes! No jet planes!"
His eyes are the shining frame
for a sky that is safe.

CLOSING TIME

After supper I drive with my son to the lake,
enter the dark cabin, the heat of summer
gone, winter crouched beneath the beds.
Floorboards shift like thin ice underfoot
as we pack the food, cover windows
with plywood sheets.
                          We walk together
to the water, a frigid moon floating there, my son
pitches a rock that makes the moonlight vanish.
He shouts in celebration, up beyond his bedtime,
but it will freeze tonight, the pipes need draining.

I turn the pressure system off, pull the hose
from cold water – it comes out stiff and brittle,
like a frozen snake. I lay it on the bank, remove
the foot-valve, watch the water gush, its sibilant rush
the only sound in the chill night – my son

is gone, I wheel around, nothing moving,
stumble down to the lake, not a wave, moon
and stars like frost motes on black water, I scrabble
up the rocks, running in darkness, call his name,
willing my voice calm, mustn't frighten him   or me,
up the porch steps, snap on cabin lights,
every room empty, I dash outside,

the stars still ice on the lake, the moon
is gone, a cloud, I know, a cloud
is all, I swing around, caraganas
derelict and motionless,
I suck in my breath to howl
his name,
                      the backhouse door
slaps shut, and here he comes,

pausing where I clutch
the porch rail, chest
heaving.
            You look away
for just an instant:
this is how it happens.

AFTER ROUND HILL

My son thought my childhood boring,
no television, no gym at King Edward School,
the girls and boys confined to different yards.

Then I took him south of town
to the valley beyond Round Hill, the hill itself
gone, landfill for the highway running south.
We walked through willows by the creek,
the valley hardly changed from thirty years before.

We pushed through red osier dogwood,
a great horned owl in a green ash above,
his steady glare on every move we made.
Beneath the Manitoba maple, its leaning trunk
black and twisted, we found the clearing,

the circle of stones, its sunken firepit,
a few remnants of charred wood.
Here, on bedrolls cushioned by piles of grass,
in grade six my friends and I first camped overnight.
I also showed my son the gravel bar

where we launched our makeshift rafts,
the path where Chick and I snared a rabbit,
the mound of dirt where Pork entered legend,
killing two gophers with a single shot
from his homemade hickory bow.

Often in the weeks afterward
I'd look up from reading and catch my son
staring at me as if he'd just discovered sight.

WITH HIS TROUSER BOTTOMS ROLLED

When I pull into the driveway, the kids come running,
shouting before I'm out of the car: "Grandpa had an accident!"
I picture my withered father at the wheel of his Plymouth
regarding the road from under the steering wheel's arc,
the car creeping through a light, slammed sideways, crushed.

"Is he okay?" "Sure, he's gonna be fine," says my daughter.
"Mom took him to the hospital. We had to wait in Emergency."
"Not for long," my son adds, breathless, "just for the x-ray.
The doctor said at his age he shouldn't be riding a bike."

What's this? My father whom I've never seen on a bicycle,
the man who took me into the park with my first two-wheeler,
told me, "Get on, you learn best by doing," and gave me a shove.

The kids say he tossed them his cane, straddled my bike, asked
for a push, wobbled across our lawn, almost across the neighbour's.

When the broken rib mends, they add, he's going to try it again.

INTIMATIONS

Striving to make them sense
their own mortality,
I gripped the shrunken head,
a rubber toy but grisly,
addressed it as Yorick,
and no gorge rose.
But after class
one boy shied towards me:
"I was just wonderin' if …well…
Howdja like a real skull for that part?"
Trying not to think
of what was left headless,
I seized upon his offer.
Now when Hamlet holds
the jester's skull,
the classroom grows
quiet as the grave.
They see the end,
and cannot laugh at that.

JOHN'S POEM

His father with a hard eye for the women,
his mother dead in an exhaust-choked car,
the coroner, at least, thought of the kids,
labelled it an accident.
But it was no accident
that John strayed.
In grade nine ranked with the wilder seniors,
quit football to work after school,
needing money for the beer and the girls.

Strange to see him in grade twelve
practising to pantomime a scene from *Hamlet*.
No mere dumb show to him.
"Awright you guys, we gotta do this right,
Anybody laughs is gonna get it."
More than threats stilled the snickers.
John knew what Shakespeare was hitting at,
and we could recognize that much.

After the Olivier film
one girl said what more were thinking.
"You know that closet scene with Ophelia?
Well, I thought John and Gaye did it better."
Little enough reward, I guess,
for having to live a part.

TRUTHS

Looking at the photographs, I'm shocked.
We were in the castle hall with Claudius posturing,
the very torches guttering at his blustering words.
Then Osric danced below his plumes
              and the duel was on.
Hamlet and Laertes caught in a faithless match,
fencing till the sweat ran, the cheers rang,
and Gertrude's eyes stuck on the poisoned cup.
No one was jarred by the flash bulb's pop.
There are no anachronisms in Elsinore
when Hamlet tears at Claudius' throat
and makes him toast union with death.

Yet all the photos show
is Don and Dallas, Paddy, Bob and Kathy,
kids in v-necks and blue jeans,
caught in fluorescent glare
between the blackboard
and rows of cluttered desks.

There must be a finer truth,
the one that we recall.

HISTORY
   for Larry Hadwen

The names have rung in his mind
since he was chosen to go,
Birkinau, Treblinka, Dachau, Auschwitz.
He is one of fifteen teachers
who walk through the gates of death,
who will walk out again.
He knows he will see the mass graves
where no names mark the place of the Jews,
the gas chambers, the ovens, the chimneys
from which their ashes fell.

Surrounded by electrified wire,
he gazes at tree-lined streets, tidy barracks.
Inside a building he walks slowly by a case of shoes,
oxfords, boots, loafers, piles of them,
most worn, the leather cracked, a few
looking as comfortable as those he now wears.
Brogans, sandals. A pair of baby booties.
He turns away. Stops.
Wonders what he's staring at.
A dark mass, black, gray, every shade of brown.
Hair, mounds of human hair. And there at the top,
the blonde braid of a child,
the ribbon still around it. And he
is weeping, the tears
like ash on his cheeks.

AT WORK

Sunday morning in the staffroom,
I'm marking grade twelve exams, a stack
nearly as high as the Bard's beard.
There's something wrong with the fifth paper.
One answer in a tight neurotic scratch
that overflows the space allowed,
but every other space is blank.
"It's just impossible," writes Matt Tyndal,
"for me to answer any of your questions.
Here's why. All I can ever think about
is your daughter. I'm so in love with her."
My daughter. In grade nine. My stomach
lurches, a sudden weight on my chest.

No, this isn't right, it's utter silliness.
She's just a kid. Her friends come round at supper-time.
While she's helping with the dishes, they perch
on the branches of our poplar tree, laughing,
making monster faces with their flashlights,
and she climbs to join them, cracking bubble gum.

More adolescent foolishness, yes, of course,
that's what it is. I set his test aside.
Have to get back to the marking. Can I
identify anything that might
approximate a right answer?
I've got to try. Come on,
focus on the writing.

Pages of scribbled responses, then
the essay question, sheets of foolscap,
explanations that amble, circle, sometimes
nail their prey.

His paper's right here.
I pick it up, contrive to hold it still.
There's something on the final page:
"It doesn't matter what you say.
I want her. I'm going to have her."

WATCHING HER

When first my daughter took the stage
for Doris Sitter's School of Dance,
the year's finale, "Every Child A Star,"
she wobbled on her toes, and waved,
her mom and I seated in the front row.
She kept dancing, learned to tap and kick,
to spin in unison with other whirling figures,
sure moves in floodlit grace, her mom and I
watching from shadows underneath the balcony.

In high school she quit the dancing
and made the mixed curling team,
told us there was one rule,
on Tuesday nights and Thursdays
we were not to enter the Hillcrest Rink.

Just once I trespassed in the lounge,
bought a beer and edged toward
windows overlooking sheets of ice.
I found the red and gold team, spied
my daughter sliding from the hack, stretching
to release — but her friend, the skip, looked up,
I ducked away, pausing a second at the bar,

my eyes shut, I see her slide, fluent and sure,
her rock skimming the ice, she rises, follows it,
watches as it strikes the shot rock, peels off
and hits another, clears the house, settles
three inches from the button. My daughter
raises her hands above her head, taps
her feet, triumphant, pirouettes and smiles,
then, yes, she's waving up at me.

WHAT THE FATHER KNOWS

He recalls his dream, in a cave
he was, going down, always down,
when he wanted to be up and out,
explosions beginning, echoes
from a darker tunnel, everything
falling, boulders all around him,
the only air – dust, and he was hacking,
gasping, startled, blackness
everywhere, hearing
                              cautious
footsteps
              padding down the hall.

The first one out of bed
he stops inside the bathroom,
a raw smell, sour, faintly nauseous,
a hint of gagging in the throat.

He closes the bathroom door
and thinks about his teenaged son,
trying everything for size.
He pictures the boy curled
here in the night – talking
on the big white telephone,
as the guys used to say. He studies
the ivory porcelain, the creamy tile,
and where they meet, a bright lump of vomit,
green, uncurling like a leaf.

GOLDEN WEST

Old men were once young, but it is uncertain
if young men will reach old age. — Democritus

A blanket of stars overhead, my girl warm
beside me in my father's Nash, John Wayne
stepping into the saddle, his gruff drawl
in a box at my ear, and rising like a grizzly
on its hind legs, another guy, bigger than Wayne,
fills the screen, a giant bucket of popcorn
hugged to his chest, one hand on the hood of our car.
He lurches away, pitches along the semi-circle ahead,
spills light from the door of a half-ton Ford, shoves
the popcorn inside, follows it in.
Finally closes the door.

His brake lights flash on and off. On again.
A horn blares behind him, his lights a furious red.
More horns. "I wouldn't try that, Pilgrim,"
says John Wayne, a smear on the screen, and I see
the half-ton's headlights are on. All around us
horns protest. Light slops from an opening door.
He lunges out, stumbles, beer bottle in hand,
clambers into the box of the truck. "Come on,"
he shouts. "Anyone who wants a good
shit-kicking, I'm the man to hand it out."

The drive-in is gone, screen torn down,
refreshment shack demolished, the poles
with the speaker boxes wrenched from the earth,
where the cars used to park, hillocks ploughed away.
The arch that said *Golden West Drive-In*
guards a field of spear-grass and weeds.
A tumbleweed leans on the sagging gate.
Wind tears at the sign that says *olde West*.

The guy in the half-ton was grabbed by the arm,
two men from the row behind dragging him down.
They pounded him till he fell, put the boots to his ribs,
left him lying beside his puddle of light, slammed
his door into darkness.

                       After a while
he sat up. Got his hand on the fender.
Managed to stand. Hauled himself
into the cab.

                I never saw him again.

THE FIRE
  for Lorna Crozier and Patrick Lane

That first summer at Fort San
she was passion, talent,
a flare awaiting the match.
"Here. You'll love these," I said,
handing her my worn copy of
Beware the Months of Fire.

A writers' conference, and they meet
in the white heat of words,
the flames spreading.
A week later he calls from the coast,
wants her number in Swift Current.
Both of them already taken, both
ready for the fire.

Then living together,
no longer two people.

One September night poets
commandeer a corner
of the Bessborough lounge,
Patrick entertaining,
stories of his ancient aunts,
"Remember when we threw
the baby in the furnace?"
Gory tales told to shock
relatives at family reunions.

And Lorna, radiant.
She reaches across his knee,
touches me. "You used to say
I'd burn out. Never make thirty.
I'm thirty-one now."
"Ah, but you've changed."
"Oh, yeah?"
Patrick leans back,
smiles, starts
another story.

MEMORIES FROM FORT SAN
for Robert Kroetsch

Writers take a break in Lipton bar.
You, beard a grizzled grey,
are the only one who'll argue
alone with Rudy Wiebe.

When he sings *Amazing Grace*
you match his baritone
with *Cigareets an' Whisky.*
And wild, wild mentors,
they write like crazy,
they keep us insane.

When Rudy's fierce roar
draws scowls from the locals,
a new waiter strides over:
"Settle down, or I throw you out."

Rudy shakes with laughter
unable to voice his excuse.
Sober as a preacher
you rise from a pulpit of booze:
"He's the only one drinking
nothing but orange juice."

Next morning in the washroom rush,
Rudy greets you, grinning,
complains of his tang-over.

MOTHER POETRY
for Anne Szumigalski

Vast woman
dances with fireflies,

a lyric whisper
light on the breeze.

Lady of culture
ponders Blake,

floating naked
where echoes speak.

Twilight quiet,
gleam of lapis lazuli,

she plans the silence
between the lines.

Her garden of words
where singing deciphers

the secrets of crickets
for bending ears.

THE MOST CREATIVE ACT

He thinks of counterpoint the
cadence of a catalectic line that breaks
another curving back upon itself the flow
into cesura's calm   texture
of vowels and consonants   expect
-ations dashed   the stretch of
tension   aesthetic   distance.

He sets himself the task:
write the poem   and   never
mention her smile

AT THE SUMMER WRITING SCHOOL

She knows he'll be a challenge.
His first poem is about a gopher
erect by its hole, the hole concealed
in a dark tangle of grass, the gopher
going in and out of the hole, in and out,
then lying limp in the sunlight.
Heavy silence after his reading.
"No one's getting it," he says,
and grins, grins like a prankster.

His second poem she saves
for their private conference.
This one's about a ghost town,
but not a shack, not a weed is real.
He's never seen grey planks aged by wind,
never walked past boarded windows.

"Your assignment," she says,
"is to go for a ride on the prairie,
find a dying town to write about."
But he hasn't a car. When she offers hers,
he can't drive. "All right then,
I'll take the afternoon, drive you myself."

"Well thanks, but I don't think so.
You'd want me to change my poem."
She stares at him a long time,
the deep intelligent eyes, wonders
what she can possibly teach him.
"Keep writing," she says, her voice calm.
"Publish whatever you can. But never,
as long as you live, never ask me
to read another word you write."

WRITERS' RETREAT
for Melanie Little

The midnight halls still thick with heat
in the friars' quarters he turns and
turns again   rumples the bed
imagines a fan's cool breath
Through eyes squeezed shut he sees
the former skater carving figures
a moonlit backyard rink
hiss of blades slicing ice sheer
form   polished   the sheen of stars

Deep in the other wing she sleeps
dark hair shines on the pillow
her resting figure's perfect
grace   one leg   limber and brown   stretches
the taut calf curves
                    away
          from double axels
                         her intricate
      life in the air
                  landings
                                  falls
            faded now   soft
as cotton   cool
on the warm sheet
          her sleep
      a faint memory of ice

while in that other room he turns
at ease and settles in   rapt by dreams
above his bed in steady cadence
his frosted breath floats and fades

DESSERT

"It doesn't matter how good the speaker is.
You have to have a treat at the end of the day. "
— Joann Deck, cook, St. Michael's Retreat

in the cool glass bed
grapes tumble together
glowing rounds of cantelope
rub against curvaceous plums
moisture beads their purple skin
strawberries nuzzle one another
nestle next to kiwi fruit
stroke a peach's russet cheek
more come-hither gestures
as juices slip together watermelon
slices slide across each other
their dark eyes wink salaciously
and   oh   oh   honeydew

find a black forest glade
moonlight rich as cream
the chocolate touch moist and firm
texture dark as midnight yes
yes the cherry's bright
tongue in my mouth

AND SOME HAVE GREATNESS THRUST UPON THEM

I never thought I'd ever achieve
greatness in sport though often I dreamt
of leading the Riders into the Grey Cup,
of pouring jumpshots over Bill Russell's head,
of replacing Willie Mays in the '54 Series,
my own legs churning, driving me back
to the wall for that game-saving catch.
Dreams, I thought, nothing but dreams,
until that night in the Palliser gym,
playing pick-up with a bunch of teachers, I drove
for the head of the key, laid a brilliant fake
on Benton the Stork, who was a head taller and suddenly
helpless, as I rose like a phoenix into the air,
burning with glory, the ball, a fire
on the tips of my fingers, launched
in that blazing arc that always ends
at the basket, the other players dazzled,
confined to the floor by more than gravity,
their mouths popped open to see
my lean body lifted above them, doing
– it's important that this be abundantly clear –
doing exactly what Michael Jordan did for the Bulls,
the luminous ball like the moon in its slow descent,
and before the wonderful sigh of cords parting
I was back on the hardwood floor, my landing
awkward, my ankle already beginning to throb.

POEM FOR A TWENTIETH ANNIVERSARY

At a conference far from home
we set out   recalling how to howl
till I brake to a stop
outside the Sutherland Hotel
Motorcycles line the sidewalk
twenty bikes that gleam like chains

I stride into the bar   hoping
the phone is near the door
Silence swings through the room
Black leather   beards
eyes like metal studs turn on me
teacher's shirt and tie   pressed slacks
only man in the room with no tattoo

    Say ...I was wondering ...uh –
    do you have a phone I could use?
He turns from pulling draught
his hand a froth of suds
    Pay phone in the lobby he says
Voices rev   a rumble of broken mufflers
I step into a different sound
where a biker chokes the phone
short nasal explosions
snap along the wires

On the floor his lady rides
his shoulder-pack   eyes closed
smoking something she has rolled
A fur halter tightens
as she drags the smoke inside
On her left breast the tattoo of a nude
whose pelvis swells obscenely

The phone crashes down
Her eyes open meet mine She says
    Go ahead, Mister. Enjoy yourself.
    I'll really make her dance.
The biker grunts a warning

                 The shock

is me dialing the phone here
now I swallow hard and
say it *I love you* words
that occupy the lobby surge
around the bikers crouched and silent
staring at my slacks
the creases razor-sharp

IT GOES SO FAST
for Ryan

In elementary school,
you dared a trampoline;
the crack, a breaking branch,
before the shock of pain,
you knew it was your leg.
I got a call at work,
rushed to the hospital,
ran out to squealing brakes,
flung the door wide, you
raising your head on the stretcher:
"Relax, Dad, it'll be okay."

In grade nine, off you went
to Thunder Bay, a youngster
at a conference, strode
through the din of strangers, shook
hands, at ease beside the keynote speaker.
Next you blocked a volleyball,
hung on to make the senior team
with throbbing swollen fingers.
In your final year jumped higher
than you knew, helped lift that team
to a provincial medal, your coach,
grinning at you, said, "He's ol' reliable."

When high school ends, you're gone,
speeding for the mountains, a job
at Lake Louise, the freedom
of a ski bum, and I, bereft
but happy too, am hopeful now
though your battered Dodge Colt
sputters, bucks and kicks
like a stallion, ripe
to hurl you at the ditch.

GOING NOW
for Bronwen

That look I see today
I know I've seen before.
You must have been two years old,
setting off down the street,

going with the neighbour girls
(the same two who tapped our door
the first day we brought you home,
already hoping you'd come out and play).

They held you tight at two,
one gripping each hand, you
tottering along on tiptoe,
willing yourself taller, turning

your head, your smile a vow, tossing
back at your mother and me
a look that said, "I'm going now.
There's a world out there." And here,

today, I'm the one you walk beside,
in the aisle a whisper of silk,
the curve of your neck, that smile again.
Another moment, oh, and you'll be gone.

Ending

THE GLOVE

A pickup game, and she wants to borrow a glove. Well, there's my old three-finger model.

A hint of mould, something stored too long, the damp shed. Like an old shoe, lace broken, leather dry as drought, tongue hanging from the open mouth. Paynton, Sask., August 1948. I shiver at the moose head, empty sockets glaring from the barn wall, but Aunt Jessie's in the kitchen with her mixing bowl, a chocolate coat of icing. Dandelion parachutes. No water in the ditch to float a raft. Elevators across the CN tracks from Joe Luke's cafe. Cherry pie on chipped white plates. Cousins, uncles eating. Bottle opener spinning on the table, and my father pays the bill. Paynton Mustangs out behind the Wheat Pool elevator. Another loss. Meteors pour beyond the dipper, spill unseen on Pilsner bottles in the dark.

Amber glow the morning after. Fortunes change, my turn will come. Prairie lilies bright as paint, and bottles in the grass, smell of warm beer. The sheen of coins. Crouching in the heat. Stow the bottles in a gunny sack. Crested wheat grass leans with wind, pointing, sunlight on red hide, a supple creature curled into the hollow.

I find it there, the three finger model, its pocket dark with oil. The sure feel on my hand. Playing catch with my father. And Sunday school picnics, Trinity Tigers go against the grown-ups, second base for the King Edward Hawks, pickup games and scrub, the writing school at Fort San, summer of '77, tournament with entry fees, second base again, the poets' gift: one incredible win.

But leather cords rot, things slip through, fall away. Decades in the shed. I take a nylon lace from the dresser. Weave it through the fingers, feel my father's leathery face, whole again, my own limber hand.

Well, maybe not.
Give her the Rawlings Fastback, hinged pad, basket web, Jose Canseco's name burnt into the palm.

AFTER THE SECOND ACT

We meet beside the bar,
the first time in a decade.

Twenty years have plunged by
since our July in Echo valley,
staccato strains scoring the hills.
You a painter, me a writer,
the two of us, that summer of music,
surviving together, artists
by day, drinkers by night, the pool
table awash with our laughter.

And then earning a living,
while the kids came, the families grew.

We shake hands, shift
into a hug, have another drink,
fill in the years, you tell me
you're teaching now,
small hand movements
to dental technicians,
the pay isn't bad. I ask,
"How's the painting? You still at it?"

Like breath from a mirror,
something fades.

I sense the skull's chill shape
brittle beneath the skin.
You shake your head, shrug,
glance sliding off.
That young man in a jean jacket,
his pocket bulging with brushes. The years
pressing between us, you drift back
toward the bar, lose yourself in the crowd.

WHY I WAS SEATED IN THE MIDLE OF THE FRONT ROW
AT THE SASKATCHEWAN CENTRE OF THE ARTS

Aunt Aggie had spent the whole morning shopping for dresses.
Tired, sick of high heels, hungrier than a hog, she
ordered spaghetti and meatballs for lunch at Alfredo's.
The waiter was Scottish and slow bringing the meal.
She hurried to get it inside her. Good food,
she always says, won't do no one no good
if it just lies like a worm on the plate.
She had arranged to meet Myrtle Belle in the mall
directly beneath the statue of the third Ukrainian lady
and she was rushing her meal when one string of spaghetti
did a jig on her fork, sprayed tomato sauce on her pink blouse.
She patted the fabric with a damp serviette,
cleaned off her plate and scurried for Eaton's,
hoping to find spot remover in Main Floor Notions.
While handing over $9.99 for a bottle
no bigger than a munchkin's thimble,
she saw the sales clerk's mouth flop open
as if she were ready to swallow a rabbit.
Aunt Aggie swung around and there,
directly across the aisle in Men's Wear,
no more than five feet away, stood
Tony Bennett, thumbing a packet of silk handkerchiefs.
"Good gravy glory me," Aunt Aggie yelped, and Tony Bennett,
compelled by the squeal in her voice, turned and found
himself staring at a seventy-six year old woman
whose blouse was bedaubed with tomato sauce.
Aunt Aggie was close enough, she could have tousled his wig.
She blushed, glanced at his packet of hankies, blurted,
"Nose rags to riches!" and ran for the mall.
It took more than a minute to catch her breath
before she told Myrtle Belle what a fool she'd been.

Tonight her living room sofa was as close
as she'd get to any concert. Holy old Hanna,
she couldn't let Tony Bennett spot her in the crowd.
There was no telling what the man might do.

UNCLE LYLE LIVES ALONE

The relatives gather at Lyle's place.
For six months now his wife
has been in a home. Alzheimer's.
"A damned shame," he says,
"she's healthy as a hog at kill time,
but her mind, you know,
it wanders, yeah, and so does she.
That last month she was here
I kept finding her outside
in the dead of night,
peeing on the marigolds
or chasing the cat that run off
twenty-three years ago.

"Damn, I wish I could trade half my brains
for just a fraction of her good health.
I try to eat, but the food won't stay down.
Skinnier than a starved-out fence rail,
I'll just float away some day."

My dad chuckles, nods. "Thank God
for the force of gravity," he adds.
"Gravity, Hell!" says Uncle Lyle.
"There's these magnetic forces
come out of your feet, holes
in the soles of your feet,
that's all that holds you down."

Abrupt silence. Everyone staring,
our breath loud, crowding the room.

"Oh," says my dad at last. "Well, uh,
I don't know if I'd believe that."
"Don't matter what you believe,"
says Lyle. "Facts is facts."

ONE OF THE GUYS
for John "Pepper" Sim

Over a quarter of a century since we've
seen each other, but always your letter
in the card arrives as sure as Christmas.

More than forty years since we hung together,
playing scrabble in your parents' living room,
inventing words no lexicon would dare.

Teammates on the Central Cyclones.
With your knee hurt, I got a chance at fullback,
saved you for the sweep that won the game.

We were members of the Bluebirds, Pep and Treb,
proud to wear our names with Searce and Flash,
Stork and Chenny, Pooner, Fuzz and Clink,

a bunch of us seizing the stage at assembly,
the wonder spreading as we sang
"Sixteen Tons" in seven different keys.

We tasted our first liquor underage, of course,
honking up our guts, patting heaving backs,
saying, It's okay, buddy, you're going to be okay.

After all the action we'd sprawl on furniture and floor,
a single light in Flash's stereo, one record turning,
"The Twelfth of Never" ringing out till dawn.

And oh, the surge of power in grade twelve
as we burst from school for Christmas holidays,
the whole main drag was ours at last.

But in the long run, Pep, I guess we had it wrong.
There'll be no card from you this year.
Nor any other.

HERE'S TO YOU, SEARCE

April grey with winter sludge
and I think of you, old friend, caught
somewhere between middle age
and the end that always follows.
The sky opens, the street
suddenly streaming, pebbles
of rain beat down,
the whole block dancing.
The window pane melts,
poles, trees waver, ripple,

and I am seventeen again,
looking out from Flash's house,
you and I caught by the downpour
that could last for hours.

"Well, time to go home," you say
and strip off shoes & socks, shirt & pants,
fold them neatly in a plastic bag,
cradle the bag like a football.

A second later you're dashing
down the centre of the street,
water splashing from your feet,
glistening on your flashing legs,
your broad shoulders. Cars
pull over, horns applaud.
You turn once, grin
at us cheering from the door,
then disappear from sight.

Somewhere beyond the rain
you walk more slowly now,
bearing whatever falls upon your back,
bent somewhat, hip replaced,
pacemaker attached, but that grin, I know,
that grin still bright somehow,
gleaming through the night.

AUDREY BANTING

I

Freshman year in the boarding house,
abruptly awake in the basement, I know
the neighbour's cat prowls the dark room,
and you, the working girl who lives upstairs,
a farmer's only child, who thinks of me,
another only child, as a younger, secret brother,
you are at the back door again, the door
propped open by your foot so you can linger,
his hands stroking your back, another impossibly
long and torrid kiss from that salesman
who always brings you home so late, the cat
a gentle current on your calf as it passes by.

II

Ten-thirty at night and the phone rings,
an old friend from college days who swears
he's just now seen the paper, damn,
he's sorry to be the one to tell me.
I try to visualize the way it was.

III

Christmas day in Royal University Hospital,
at the nursing station a solitary nurse selects
a chocolate, scribbles on a chart, glances
toward your door, the weight uncurled already
from your chest, a fluent leap from the bed, padding
on the tiles, the door swung open, the advancing nurse
doesn't notice the subtle charge that for a second
draws her skirt away from her calves,
doesn't know that you are gone.

FOR MARY DROVER

I

Lamentation's not her style.
She'd never tell you she's had cancer,
had it, yes, had it, and had it again.
She must be troubled by a knee
that always buckles, crutches
that people no longer even notice,
parts of herself that are gone.

You wouldn't hear her say it though.
She comes to work the same as usual,
carries on the way she always did,
brief showers of laughter
that make the moments shine.

II

Awkward on my broken foot, I pause
beneath the single flight of stairs,
hand off one crutch to a friend,
take my weight on the other, stretch
for a grip on the railing, pull
and hoist, pull and hoist,
make my way up the stairs.

A second later Mary swings into view,
her crutches visible once more.
"Oh, Mary, have I got a new appreciation for you!"
But she shakes her head and waves me off.
"Hey, I wear a bag around my neck
just to carry things." She grins and says,
"And how do you bag a cup of coffee?"
We gripe and laugh together.
For a moment now she's free.

III

I approach her friends from far and near,
exchange hugs ardent as our memories.
The coffin in the next room, we can talk
of other rooms, the wine flowing late
in hotel rooms after meetings, moments
burnished by her wit, bursts
of laughter now, the ache
unseen inside.

GZOWSKI IN THE HEARTLAND

The Harwood, his old watering hole, is gone,
but at least he's back in Moose Jaw
where he started forty years before.
In Peacock Centennial Auditorium
the crowd, shocked to find him six feet tall,
soon relaxes; Peter's bearded, rumpled,
as cozy as a favorite sweater.
He talks about community, the way
that meanings warp, he chuckles
at news blips about the nudist community,
the bankruptcy community, the blast
that sent shivers through the terrorist community.
In Canada, the Red River Rally brought
genuine communion, people reaching out
turned the country to a neighbourhood.
"We do," he says, "huddle together against the cold."

In the warmth of the jammed auditorium,
eight hundred souls are held by lies and memory:
– the five Ks he runs each day, then pushups,
and a raw halibut before the drive to work;
– his argument with Stuart McLean
that the pet cricket arrived at work
already dead; no, it did not expire
from his second-hand tobacco smoke;
– his probing of Pierre Trudeau who always
stayed three steps ahead, the only P.M.
who could recite "The Love Song
of J. Alfred Prufrock," or wanted to;
– the accident just before he and his co-host
go on air live, a flagon of boiling tea
spilled into his lap; "Excuse me, Maggie," he says,
drops his drawers, and does the show.

Then the questions he'd rather no one asked:
What have you accomplished? Are you happy with yourself?
The shrug, the fumbled phrase, the mumbled line
that everybody knows leads so often to the truth.
"Well," he says at last, "I'm good at what I do."
The Peacock crowd roars in deep accord,
Gzowski held in the heart of the heartland,
the final word from a young woman
speaking to her friend who every morning
brought the country to her kitchen.
Now she asks what others want to know:
"Peter, when will you be coming by for tea?"
In the crowd of prairie people, we all feel
somehow it should be possible.

A LITERARY MOMENT

Nerves jerking, lack of sleep, everything
on edge, or overload, excitement
of working on the Festival of Words, I dash
for the car as applause engulfs
Jane Urquhart, vibrant at the podium, I gun
it for Regina, the Hotel Sask., wonder
if I can do this, make it through all right.
Up three flights of stairs, rasping breath,
Writers' Guild employees waiting in the library.

Weren't they in Moose Jaw when I left?
They laugh and shake their heads, tell me
it will be a minute yet, then
they'll hand me over to Cindy.
I fall into a seat, spray
small talk in five directions,
fingers jumping on my knees.

                    A door opens,
a lovely woman flows into the room,
her limber shape the kind that evening
gowns are made to cling to. "And now,"
she says, "you're all mine." Sudden warmth
takes my hand, leads me to an empty chair,
slides into another facing me, her calf
a fever next to mine. Full lips, lustrous red,
open slowly. "Take off your clothes," she says.
                    What's this?
There are people in the room. "Uh, pardon me?"
"Take off your glasses, please."

Oh. Yes, of course. I hand them to her, sparks
leap between our fingers, her fingers
cool on my forehead, cheekbones,
the bridge of my nose, her thumbs
pressing my upper lip, fingers rubbing
my chin, stroking the line of my jaw,
the cords of my neck, kneading, soothing,
knots unwinding, lines wiped away, building
a foundation, dabbing make-up, massaging it in,
concealer here, shadow there, a touch of blush,
fingers dance, smooth my eyebrows, a dusting
of powder, soft bristles graze, caress...

      I think I may be sleeping
but someone says, "Now, I'll walk you in."
I'm in a library, there are other people here.
I raise my arm. "No, no," she says, her voice
dark and lyrical. "I'll walk *you* in. It's *your* time."
My hand on her arm, I'm wafted through the doorway.

Cables running everywhere, television cameras,
tripods, banks of lights, reflector screens,
sound technicians, camera men. The director
has decided he will tape all three selections,
no rehearsals, no instructions, no advice.

No matter. I'm floating high above it all.
We do three poems in three takes, thank you, Cindy,
then the final shot, stroll across the room,
place my toes in the "T" that's taped on the rug,
gaze eight inches past the lower camera,
say, "My name is Robert Currie."
That one requires another take.

GREEN/YELLOW/RED

I meet her in the middle of Main Street,
pause to talk; her smile that could stop traffic
doesn't: two lines of cars are launched toward us,
we continue talking, engines gunning for us as
we step onto the traffic island, hands gesturing,
I feel a blast sweep beneath my left wrist,
the mirror on a half-ton hurtles by, burning
rubber, exhaust fumes, a broken muffler's roar.

I tell her a story of Thomas King: he's in this Men's Wear
on Yonge Street, delighted to discuss the latest Giller winner
with a clerk who's read it too. Glad to be gone from Chapters
where no one knows which book won. King admits
he probably isn't being fair. The Chapters staff, heck,
they maybe know a lot about men's fashions.
"It sounds exactly like him," she says,
"that dry sense of humour."

The lights have changed, and another woman
steps onto the island, yet another right behind her.
The first one looks surprised – and pleased.
"You're Mr. Currie," she says, touching my arm.
"You used to be my teacher!" Her eyes
expand. "And you're Shelagh Rogers. Oh,
I miss you so much on *Take Five*."
"Ah," says Shelagh, "but it was just
an empty studio. Never anyone to talk to."

On a concrete island, four people locked
in conversation, the world around us
rushing somewhere else.

A DAY NO PIGS WOULD DIE

Instead the man who killed them, dead,
his son finding him in the barn
where he'd exiled himself,
a cough wrenching their nights.
The boy was thirteen years old,
but his father, who killed for a living,
had taught him of life and death.
He made the arrangements,
did the chores,
and before sundown
the clods of dirt
had drummed briefly
on the wooden box,
echoing through silent woods.
And then there was nothing to do
but walk away from the mound
of fresh earth.

I close the book.
Gwen asks, "How was it?"
and mumbling, "Okay,"
I leave the room
so she won't see
the tears that well
for a gentle man
whose job was killing pigs
and for a father
I will one day
lower to the earth
and for me
with my kids
looking
down.

READING TOGETHER

"Help, help, a Horrible Heffalump!
Hoff, hoff, a Hellible Horralump!"
I'm gasping with laughter, unable to read,
my daughter and I clutching our sides
as that bear of little brain blunders again
while Piglet runs for his life.

Now she has children of her own
and I read from richly colored picture books.
The same blonde hair and shining face,
but it's my granddaughter who snuggles close,
both of us bewitched by words.

My daughter watches us, side by side,
a man of sixty, a child of three.
She hands me another book,
hard-covered, fat as any novel.
"Marin," she says, "what should Grandpa read?"
Marin grinning wider, wiggles with pleasure.
"Chapter five," she says,
"in which Piglet meets a Heffalump."

She knows she's got it right,
all three of us grinning now
like Pooh before a honey pot.

RUNNING

My body once was lath-lean except
for shoulder blades, ankle bones, knees
like knobs beneath the skin, but I could run
from the boys' door to home plate
so fast I'd be the first to bat,
then I'd lay down a crummy little
bunt and beat the throw to first.

One time my friends and I ran in darkness,
the school yard charmed, ran because we'd rung
the bell on Mr. Keenan's door, and he could
run too, but in the shelter of the night
he was not as fleet, the base lines
lost in shadow, the ground so low
it couldn't reach my feet which flew
so fast I knew for sure at any second
I would simply disappear.

And disappear I did,
though someone much like me
sits solid on my daughter's couch,
his grandson curled against his paunch,
listening to a tale about a little boy,
a neighbour girl — it's *Yuck! A Love Story*,
but there's a dog who runs like a palomino colt,
and Brendan rises from my side to show me,
races in a circle through hallway, kitchen,
dining room, he's past me and gone again,
just four years old and travelling so fast
I fear already he's begun to disappear.

ALMOST BEDTIME

At two and four, together in the tub, otter
sleek, Joel and Jayden squeal and splash,
raise geysers with their mouths,
threaten to drink the tub dry.

Half-dried, giggling, they shake
a spray of silver beads from their hair,
drop their towels, run naked down the hall. Disappear.
Two ghosts in the curtains, they wait,
until I'm almost settled on the couch, then
the haunting, one after the other, they hurl themselves
toward me, screaming and laughing, into my arms
and out, again, again, curtains streaming,
and then it's quiet time.

Jayden picks a favourite book, *Happy Birthday, Moon*,
which she says she can read all by herself.
When Bear's gift of a top hat tumbles off the moon,
she says, "The hat's all grundgley now. Bear's going home
for megredients. He'll be back in a confusey. He's going
to make the moon a chocolate peanutbutter nut cake."

Meanwhile, Joel is busy on the floor, dropping names.
"Baby Old MacDonald," he says, "Neptune, Monet,
Mozart, Shakespeare, Vinci, Guyayeo, Baby Aminals."
Like blocks, he stacks his "deedleydee" cases,
pulls their liners out and puts them back again,
restacks the pile and pats it till it's perfect.

Time for bed. A poem's the promise that I keep,
and who can say where dreams will lead them next?
Or will they sleep in lovely woods, dark and deep?

READING IN BED
   for Gwen

Should've doused the light an hour ago,
but Rumpole's on a romp through the old Bailey,
badgered too by She Who Must Be Obeyed
until I'm almost half-asleep,
                    asleep   falling
through laughing leaves   a Manitoba maple
drifting up   branch on swaying branch   the book
slipping from my hand   I clutch it
hold   a slippery pitcher by the handle
   tilting   pouring silver liquid
words showering *argentum flicker vermillion*
spillikin bamboo lover   the pitcher
sliding down a silver river slipstream
of sibilance *Susquehanna susurration*
Ahhh Susanna sustentation   pitcher
turning slowly languid –
Thump!   My eyes jerk open   see
you   snapped from sleep   blinking
eyes   dark and wide   now   like
your expansive smile
mmm spacious special sustenance

BRUSHING MY HAIR

Lying among the firm bristles of my hairbrush
like snakes in stubble, three hairs, grey and thin.
I duck my head before the bathroom mirror,
gaze above my glasses at the white sheen of flesh,
nodules of water quivering from the damp brush,
the underbelly of a bottom-feeder wrenched
from a tangle of weed in a warm lake.

I grip the hairbrush in my right hand,
propel it in slow, deliberate strokes
sweeping back from forehead to neck,
grey hairs falling away, dropping out, they
pull themselves free, leap for the brush,
in moments my hair depleted – all of it gone.

The brush now a pliant pad of grey continues
with firm and even strokes, no longer brushing,
rubbing, it polishes and buffs, my head bright
as the greased biceps of a power-lifter,
shining, smooth and brown, like the catcher's mitt
which the coiled pitcher studies as he winds up
for the final strike of a perfect game.

NOT A NICE DAY

It's noon, and I've finished my forty laps,
I'm doing stretches at the edge of the pool
– my right leg's always ready to cramp –
when I look down at my calf and notice my swimsuit,
its colour washed out, fabric transparent.
I plunge under the water – oh,
          my balding head,
                    chest hair turning grey,
but the hair on my balls shines curly and black,
the crack of my ass on public display.

Seizing a deep breath, I swim to the ladder,
                    hang there,
a noose of ripples around my neck.
I wait and wait for the deck to clear.
Then burst from the pool, grab
a paddleboard from the rack,
hold it over my crotch, zip by
the lifeguard at ease on her stool,
switch the board around to cover my butt
and rush for the shower room, glancing
over my shoulder.
                    Nobody looking.
"Have a nice day."
                    It's the other guard,
slim and shapely and coming toward me, oh
man, my privates exposed, my face aflame. She's
the young one we all like to flirt with

and she doesn't notice a thing.

FATHER AT EIGHTY-EIGHT

Years ago he told me,
"You know, when I was young
I played on the baseball team."
But all my life he used a cane.

Now the cane shakes in his right hand.
Beneath his left shoulder, a crutch
helps him shuffle out, shove
one foot past the other to the curb
where he waits for Amil's Taxi.

His driver's license went last spring.
He failed two tests in a month,
told my mom, "What's the point?
They say I make a fair right turn.
That's it. Where in hell can you get
just making right turns?"

The taxi eases to a stop.
The driver knows what's required,
lifts arthritic legs inside.

At the Co-op, my father
heaves the car door open,
gets one hand on the roof,
swings himself to the right,
drops his legs onto pavement,
hoists his body upright, maneuvers
crutch and cane into position,
takes five steps away, stops,
pushes shut the door,
the sound like a bone
snapping on icy concrete.

All my life he used a cane.
He said once, "You know,
I used to love stealing bases."

OBJECT OF AFFECTION

The wood is grey-blonde, bone-hard,
the handle rubbed sleek as ivory.
Two dark knots stare from the shaft,
their gaze as steady as my father's eyes.

I store it beneath the bed
where it lies still, its head
curled back as if to watch
whatever came toward it.
The rubber tip is faded now, more grey
than green, one tiny pebble embedded
in the outer groove of its Nev-a-slip tread.

At the stockyards all the men had canes.
They used them to separate cattle,
to drive steers into the sales ring,
beat them toward the slaughterhouse chute.
My father hung his cane on the corner
of his desk and kept the books for the Livestock Pool.

This winter when the cast came off my broken foot,
I used his cane for a week, feeling foolish, my gait
already smoother than his awkward lurch,
one hip shot, right leg inches shorter than the left.
Ah, but my hand was on the wood that his had held,
the hook that once snapped tight around my neck.

I was hurt and crying, hot tears and curses.
"Let's see about this," he said, the cane swinging
toward me, the hook snagging me beneath the chin,
hard wood on my neck, its unyielding embrace,
as, hand over hand, he hauled me in.
He took me in his husky arms and held me,
his touch like rough stone warmed by sunshine
when his lips brushed my wet cheek.

LAST THINGS

Pop heaves himself up, leans on his walker.
"Better get started for the dining hall," he says.
"I move a tad slower than the two of you."
Mom nods at me. "You leaving now?"
"No. I'll wait and walk you down."

Her eyes rove around the room.
Two easy chairs from home,
her oak night table, the myrtlewood lamp
that Uncle John turned on his lathe,
the Hurley painting of a prairie town
like the one where she was raised, a photo
of her sisters, the handmade patchwork quilt that stretches
over two hospital beds drawn together
masquerading as a double bed.

She doesn't look at the metal dresser.
"Not much like home," she says. "Two weeks
and I'm not used to it. Maybe never will be."
I shrug, wish I knew what to say.
"Some of these people...they're strange.
There's a woman who cuddles a rubber doll."
She glances at the hall. "Both of them in diapers."

Her glance settles on the bed, lingers
there, her skin pale blue,
diaphanous beneath the eyes.
"Ready for supper?" I ask.
"Want me to wheel you down?"
She shifts her glance, stares at me,
her eyes dry, not quite focussed.
"Too tired to decide?" I ask.
A slow grin. "No, too silly, I guess."
Just that, and "Thanks for the ride,"
the last words I'll ever hear her speak.

HOLDING HER

The morning of the telephone call
I'm told that this may well be it
and hurry to the nursing home.

We find her eyes closed,
her breathing shallow, hoarse.
Pop and I sit on either side of the bed,

each of us grips a hand, murmurs
reassurances, holding her here.
"We're right beside you, Mom, right here."

"We're staying here. I love you, hon."
Words of solace shower her, variations
echoing, hardly heard by us,

as we listen to her breathing.
Quick, uneven inhalations
continuing, a deeper breath,

and another, a faint rattle in the throat,
the sound like a snake, groggy with sunshine,
startled, shaking out a warning.

Her eyes flicker in alarm, relax
once more, and we are alone.

HE LOVED TO HEAR HER PLAY

Sometimes at night my mother appears in the old house,
lingering a while by the long wall in the living room

where the upright Heintzman piano stood
the year my aunt was gone and loaned it to her.

A pale glimmer of light from the corner streetlamp
illuminates a grey pillow on the chesterfield,

but black and white ivory keys remain invisible
as they would be if they were here in darkness,

the piano long ago reclaimed and gone
– who knows where so many years after? –

my mother drawing a straightback chair toward the wall,
settling on it, her back arched, hands extended, rising,

she begins to play, agile fingers gentle on the keys,
the music, slow and elegant, an old–time waltz, perhaps,

dark figures gliding through the living room, a stately circle,
measured steps guided by lamplight, faces lit an instant as they turn,

familiar faces, relatives I haven't seen in ages,
some I only recognize from photographs,

grandparents, so many aunts and uncles, all of them
in pairs tonight, swaying to the rhythm

of the tune my mother plays my father,
a melody he may not hear again for years.

AFTERWARDS

Unloading the lower drawer of your dresser,
beneath a folded shawl, a sachet of perfume
– the sudden aroma of lavender –
and I discover your diary, which falls
open to the week of your wedding,
the paper translucent, handwriting
pale but clear, the words
dissolving before me, Mom,
as I apprehend you'll never
again read them yourself.

THREE A.M.

Awakened once more in twisted sheets,
wind mourning around the house,
I hear that rattle in your throat.
Switch on every light as I go, room
by room, but all the rooms are empty.

I pause by the sink, the tap running cold,
swallow water like winter, douse
the lights, shiver at the kitchen window,
stand and stare through chill moonlight:
garbage cans rattling at the battered fence.

WATCHING THE WORLD SERIES

The Blue Jays beaten long ago,
Pop and I watch the Series anyway, enjoy
the plays: the long throw from third
to stretch the man at first;
the catcher, planted at the plate,
bursting up, the ball a silver string to second;
the centre fielder, ignited by the crack of bat,
his uniform a brilliant blaze on green
until, just before the fence, he turns,
flares high, consumes the shining ball;
the whirling symmetry of two men
who work with angle and velocity, improvise
their double play geometry. All of it
so good to watch and yet

what we're waiting for comes later
with the final game's final out:
grown men, cynics and sophisticates,
millionaires and journeymen,
freed from gravity, launched
into the autumn air, lifted carefree,
bounding, hugging one another,
tumbling in groups upon the turf,
their smiles, their faces fierce with glee, the joy
so rarely seen in other men, who have, perhaps,
more claim to think they've surely earned –
not fame – but some degree of cheer.

EVENING AT EXTENDICARE

Seven o'clock. The dining hall swept clean,
tables pushed away, I maneuver my father
into a hushed semi-circle of wheelchairs.
Other residents sit stiffly on benches and
dinner chairs in rows before the open floor,
before the band, Andy's Midnight Combo.

In fluorescent glare, "By the Light of the Silvery Moon,"
the band plays, a thin vocalist, his quavering voice
held fast by the violin that rises, falls behind him.
"Jeepers Creepers," "Yes Sir, That's My Baby,"
"Wrap Your Troubles in Dreams," and two women
walk into each other's arms, begin to sway.
Nursing aides look for others who can waltz,
lead them to the floor, launch into the old songs.
"Let Me Call You Sweetheart." One wheelchair
is rolled before the band, turning slowly with the tune.
My father's fingers drumming leather arms,
he leans toward me. "We could do that," he says.

I stand, feel people watching me,
feel a blush crawl above my collar, shrug,
wheel him forward, step awkwardly behind,
and we enter the cluster of dancers,
my cheeks flaming. "Ain't We Got Fun?"
        But I can do this.
I slap my feet in rhythm,
                        swing him
                to the left,
                            the right,
                spin him in a circle
            at the center of the floor.

The music holds the old smile on his face
and all at once I think that I remember
a smiling man, a child at someone's wedding dance,
the child lifted through the lilting air, held firmly,
the man gliding over shining floors, graceful loops,
his slim legs stepping, reaching, closing,
the child laughing in his arms,
and somewhere beyond, a lush violin.
"I Can't Give You Anything But Love."

POSSESSIONS

Legs white as lilies in the driveway's disarray,
a woman, slim and attractive, steps quickly
by the five-speed bicycle, the pair of homemade stilts.
She doesn't hesitate at my mother's last possessions,
the cushioned easy chair from the nursing home,
the blue mikado vase, the tray of costume jewelry
destined for the Sally Ann or the nuisance grounds.
She barely glances at the box of baseball caps,
the old gas can for my father-in-law's motor-boat
(the boat itself sold when he died a dozen years ago).
She is older than I, this woman I've never seen before,
and seems intent on something more than
assorted lawn ornaments, or sprinkler heads.
"You don't remember me," she says.
"We used to sleep together."

Behind me, I sense my wife raising her head
from where she's pricing mason jars with masking tape.
The woman laughs, a sweet forgiving sound.
"You were three," she says. "We lived across from you
– when your dad ran the U.G.G. elevator in Furness."

The family across the tracks had kids, I know,
but I can't remember their names or number.
Was she the one who told me how an old hound dog
dragged itself behind the elevator annex
and crawled way underneath? The same one
who took me by the hand, led me around back?
There I dropped to my knees on the gravel,
stones sharp as crushed glass on bare skin,
but I didn't care, ducking my head to gape.
Pilings, broken bottles, empty beer cases,
and farther back a still dark mound, darker
even than shadow, a smell pushing toward me,
thick and rotten, clogging my nostrils.

The girl I used to sleep beside,
and all I remember of her and her family
is that smell, that solitary mound.

WHAT WE LEAVE BEHIND

Lying on a table in the archives, a sepia print from 1917,
the Central Collegiate football team in a line before the school,
eighteen players in what look like hockey socks, khaki pants
cropped above their knees, shoulder pads sewn outside their jerseys,
they stand with arms crossed upon their chests,
a few with hands on hips, all glaring at the future
where I look back more than eighty years later.

On that field where I learned to rush a quarterback,
they threw their blocks and ran, twenty years before my birth,
and there, stolid in the centre of the print, their coach,
his ample jaw thrust over white shirt and tie,
dark suit wrapped around his barrel chest, already
rugged as a tank, and in the fifties "Tank" was what we called him,
Mr. Ballard, our principal, who one cold October day
nailed me with detention, threatened to kick me off the team
for working out at noon hour, off-limits in the gym.

Broader than his wide shoulders the bell tower rises
over him, over the three stories of the school,
the houses marching out of focus up the hill
down which every day I drive, slipping by the building
which decade after decade was my larger home,
where I taught more than three thousand students,
brilliant and perverse, friendly, troubled, oh so very human,
our lives merged for a season in the shimmer of their youth,
and now I accelerate through the long shadow of the school
where today not a single student knows my voice, my face.

PUBLIC READING

My first and only novel's out at last, the story
of a rookie teacher struggling to survive,
its early drafts written with emotion's potent hand.
The Moose Jaw and District Reading Council
invite me to read at Empire Elementary School.
My lectern is a music stand in the library.
Metal stacking chairs hold an audience of
twenty-nine: some Central grads, former colleagues,
faces I've never seen before, a few I should recall.
Michelle from my '88 creative writing class
does the introduction. A teacher now, she
wanted to be a model, could be a model still.
She has me so relaxed, the reading flows,
a mountain stream sliding over polished stones,
laughter sparkling in the current. Leslie thanks me,
class of '95, a hard and willing worker I admire.
People gather over coffee, chat together.
Someone says, "That basement room, you know,
was his room. How much of this you think is true?"
Al – was he late '70s or early '80s? – wants a book
signed for his son who goes to Central now.
One woman, well into her 50s I suppose, approaches,
smiles – could it be I've seen this smile before?
She's from the class of '68 and wonders if just
possibly I might remember helping her with speeches.
A shiver through my chest. Oh Marilyn, I remember.
And now I wonder: has there ever been a reading
that made a writer feel as good as this?

IN THE PRESENCE OF BOOKS
for my father

Often, haunted, lost in bookstores,
I slide by the noise of mass market paperbacks,
run my fingers over cloth-bound spines,
gaze upon solemn jacket photographs,
ruffle pages, the crisp feel, the rough edges,
take in that satisfying smell
that only emanates from certain books.

Then I'll spot a volume you would prize.
The Englishman's Boy by Guy Vanderhaeghe,
the mania of Hollywood but laced with prairie facts,
a crisis in the Cypress Hills you love.
A Jackie Robinson bio, the grace
of an authentic hero, yes, the hero
of comic books you once bought a boy
so he'd learn some truths of black and white.

Two books just right for you, and in that flash
before I dip my hand toward my wallet,
I remember, your reading days
are done, Pop, and here I stand,
lost and looking down, the books
shaking in my hand.

MY FATHER'S SHOES

They lie discarded in the hall closet
where they were tossed some years ago,

the pair of Rockports, a discontinued style,
leather more orange than brown, worn soles,

pushed down heels, folded and split.
I lift and hold the shoes a moment,

stroke the furrowed leather, set them down
and slip them on, shocked to feel

how well they fit. I note a darker polish
over stains which show like pentimento,

or like the fading figure of a man
who walks away, never looking back,

though he pauses once in falling snow.

Acknowledgements:

Some of these poems – occasionally in earlier versions or with different titles – have previously appeared in the following magazines: *Canadian Author, Canadian Forum, Faces, Fiddlehead, Grain, Grey Borders, Other Voices, Prairie Fire, Salt,* and *This Magazine.* Others were published in the following anthologies: *Because You Loved Being A Stranger* (Harbour Publishing), *Draft* (Turnstone Press), *Going for Coffee* (Harbour Publishing), *Hamlet with Related Readings* (International Thomson Publishing), *I Want To Be The Poet of Your Kneecaps* (Black Moss Press), *Losers First* (Black Moss Press), *Number One Northern* (Coteau Books), *The Place My Words Are Looking For* (Bradbury Press), *The Wascana Poetry Anthology* (CPRC.), and *Where Is The Voice Coming From?* (Vol. III, SWG).

"Starting Out Together" won first prize for poetry in the 2004 Saskatchewan Writers Guild literary competition judged by Roo Borson. Both "Closing Time" and "Campus Party" won prizes in the 2005 competition judged by Susan Musgrave.

"Poem for a Twentieth Anniversary" is reprinted from *Learning on the Job* by permission of Oberon Press. This poem was included in the dramatic piece, *Tabloid Love,* which was directed by Gaye Burgess and performed by the Poets' Combine for the "Gathering the Voices" Conference which brought together writers from Saskatchewan, Manitoba, Minnesota and North Dakota, as well as for the national convention of the Canadian Conference of Teachers of English, the National Book Festival and as a fundraiser for the Sage Hill Writing Experience.

Six poems under the title of "What We Leave Behind" were staged by Angus Ferguson for the Globe Theatre's *On the Line* series in Regina. Another sequence of seven poems was staged under the title of "Father and Son" by the same director for the same series. That sequence was also produced by Kelley Jo Burke and broadcast on "Gallery" by the CBC. A somewhat different series of father and son poems was filmed by Donna Caruso for broadcast as part of her "Story Album" series on SCN. "Gzowski in the Heartland" was broadcast on CBC's "The Afternoon Edition" at the time of Peter Gzowski's death.

A few of the poems are reprinted from the following chapbooks: *Sawdust and Dirt* (Fiddlehead), *The Halls of Elsinore* (Sesame Press), and *Moving Out* (Coteau Books).

My thanks to the editors, publishers, directors, and producers who helped bring these poems to a larger audience.

Special thanks to the members of the Poets' Combine (Paul Wilson, Bruce Rice, Judith Krause, Gary Hyland and Byrna Barclay) for years of encouragement and enlightened criticism. Thanks, also, to Don McKay for his trenchant comments about earlier drafts of some of these poems and to my editor, Geoffrey Ursell, for his poetic insights, his wisdom in seeing the larger picture, and his generous spirit.

Additional thanks to Anne Warriner, Karon Selzer and the staff of the Moose Jaw Public Library for their generous assistance and for the provision of a congenial place to write and think.

The epigraph from Dylan Thomas originally appeared in an interview conducted by Harvey Breit and published in *The New York Times* on February 17th, 1952.

PHOTO: LARRY HADWEN

About the Author

Robert Currie is a poet and fiction writer who lives in Moose Jaw. His previous poetry collections include *Diving Into Fire, Yarrow, Learning on the Job, Klondike Fever,* and four poetry chapbooks. *Diving Into Fire* was a finalist for the 1977 Commonwealth Poetry Prize. His published fiction includes the novel *Teaching Mr. Cutler,* and the short story collections *Night Games* and *Things You Don't Forget.*

His stories and poems have appeared in over 40 magazines and anthologies, and he has served as either editor or co-editor for fourteen books. He also taught creative writing for four summers at the Saskatchewan School of the Arts at Fort San, Saskatchewan.

Robert Currie was born in Lloydminster, but moved to Saskatoon and then to Moose Jaw. He taught at Central Collegiate in Moose Jaw for 30 years before retiring in 1996 to pursue his writing career full time. In 1991, he was named one of the city's two poet laureates.